At the Heart of Christ

12 Days of Stories and Meditations

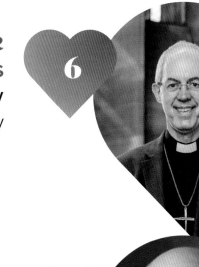
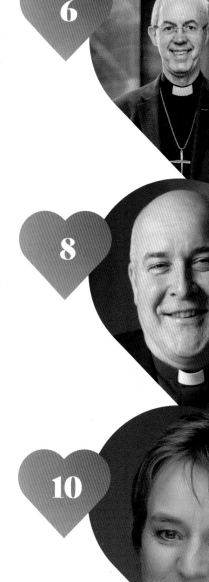

29 December
Mystery
Rachel Treweek
is the Bishop of Gloucester

14

30 December
Peace and Justice
Krish Kandiah
is a social entrepreneur,
theologian and author

16

New Year's Eve
Help for Those in Need
Gina Radford
is a vicar in Devon, having been
Deputy Chief Medical Officer
for England

18

New Year's Day
Giving Thanks
Matt Baker
is National Director for England
for Sports Chaplaincy UK and
Chaplain at Charlton Athletic FC

20

3 January
Rest and Restoration
Jamie Jones-Buchanan
played Rugby League for
Leeds Rhinos for 22 years where
he is now Assistant Coach

22

4 January
Carols
Alexander Armstrong
is a Classic FM presenter
and Cathedral Music Trust
Ambassador

24

5 January
Giving and Receiving
Tosin Oladipo
is Chaplain to the
Archbishop of Canterbury

26

6 January (The Epiphany)
Journeys
Jo Kelly-Moore
was recently announced as
the new Dean of St Albans

28

CHRISTMAS EVE

The Birth of Jesus

by Archbishop Justin Welby

This Christmas I will be remembering the words of the famous hymn –

'What can I give Him, Poor as I am?
If I were a shepherd, I would bring a lamb;
If I were a Wise Man, I would do my part;
Yet what I can I give Him: Give my heart.'
Christina Rossetti

The heart is a funny thing. Of course, it's the organ that pumps blood around our bodies, keeping us alive. But it's come to mean far more to us. The heart means our very core, our being. It's at once deeply human and visceral, yet metaphorical and transcendent. It anchors us to our mortality, but it also lifts us to our creativity, our inspiration, the relationships that we form and the people we love.

The heart is where humanity seems to meet divinity.

Reading Matthew 1.18-23

Now the birth of Jesus the Messiah took place in this way ... an angel of the Lord appeared to Joseph in a dream and said, 'Joseph, son of David, do not be afraid to take Mary as your wife, for the child conceived in her is from the Holy Spirit. She will bear a son, and you are to name him Jesus, for he will save his people from their sins.' All this took place to fulfil what had been spoken by the Lord through the prophet: 'Look, the virgin shall conceive and bear a son, and they shall name him Emmanuel', which means, 'God is with us.'

Reflection

At Christmas, God himself becomes human. His real, living heart beats; as a frail child in a cold manger he takes his first breaths on this earth. And he takes on this very human heart because of his love for you. Having a heart means experiencing heartbreak: it means knowing pain and sorrow. But it also means joy, love, hope and the promise of life. Most of all, it means relationship. In becoming human, God showed his heart isn't impervious to our lives. God doesn't watch us coldly from afar; he is here this Christmas, with us.

We often dress Christmas up, adding all the trimmings: a tree, presents, lights, food and fun. These things are wonderful, but they are not the heart of Christmas. The only thing that makes Christmas perfect is Jesus, who sees, loves, and welcomes all. The only thing we need to give him – and each other – is our hearts, our very own selves.

Wherever and whoever you are, you too are welcome and invited this Christmas, to worship the child, the God whose heart beats for you.

Where might you find space and stillness in the coming days of Christmas to listen for the heartbeat of God's love?

Day 2

CHRISTMAS DAY

Feast

by Archbishop Stephen Cottrell

Christmas is what the church calls a feast day. Consequently, my favourite bits of Christmas are all to do with eating and drinking.

I love Midnight Mass. It feels right to be celebrating the birth of Christ in the dark of the night. But Holy Communion also feels like the right way to celebrate Christmas, breaking bread and sharing wine in remembrance not just of Jesus' birth, but of his whole life, ministry, death and resurrection.

Then I love Christmas dinner the next day. I love the theatre of the table beautifully set, of food lovingly prepared, and of fine wine being drunk. I love the traditions that accompany the food; so if I have my way we'll eat a goose, there will be a flaming figgy pudding, Christmas crackers will be pulled, paper hats worn and silly jokes told.

Best of all, those I love the best will – I hope and pray – be with me round the table.

Reading Psalm 63.5-6

I will bless you as long as I live
and lift up my hands in your name.
My soul shall be satisfied, as with marrow and fatness,
and my mouth shall praise you with joyful lips ...

Reflection

As I think back over all the Christmas Eucharists I've attended and the many Christmas dinners I've eaten, two things stand out. First, I remember Holy Communion shared with those in difficult circumstances, such as Christmas visits to prison, or visiting people in hospital, or taking Communion to someone who was sick or housebound or alone.

Then I also remember the year I spent Christmas with my brother when his super-expensive, very free-range turkey that was supposed to be delivered on Christmas Eve never arrived. We made do with sausages and stuffing and roast potatoes and still had ourselves a feast.

It turned out that what really mattered was what we brought to the feast ourselves, not what was on the table in front of us. Therefore, it is me and you coming with empty hands to the altar rail on Christmas night to receive bread from heaven; and then gathered with those we love and gathering in those who have no one to love them, that is the heartbeat and meaning of our Christmas feasting.

Whom do you know who might be alone at Christmas?
What could you do to reach out to them?

Could you make some festive food to share with others in your community?

Day 3

27 DECEMBER

Good News of Great Joy

by Katherine Dienes-Williams

Across the world, time zone by time zone, packed churches resound with singing as we rejoice in the birth of Christ. Beyond the open doors of our churches people watch over flocks, people are homeless, in need, pain, or trauma. Everywhere, angels pierce the darkness, acclaiming their 'Gloria' to shepherds. In carol services, choirs like the one I direct at Guildford Cathedral rise to highest heavens, descants abounding.

Every year I look forward to singing carols for patients and staff at the Royal Surrey Hospital which is visible from the west door of the cathedral. Twenty years ago I had just given birth to our child and left hospital on Christmas Day. I had been sung to by my own choristers the night before as they came singing round hospital wards. And on this day three years ago, my mother developed sepsis and was blue-lighted to hospital. The final days of Advent and the feast days of Christmas are days when Christ's birth bringing eternal love jostles with the trials of human life as sheep jostle in fields. Yet, through it all, the Lord is our shepherd.

Reading Luke 2.8-14

In that region there were shepherds living in the fields, keeping watch over their flock by night. Then an angel of the Lord stood before them, and the glory of the Lord shone around them, and they were terrified. But the angel said to them, 'Do not be afraid; for see—I am bringing you good news of great joy for all the people: to you is born this day in the city of David a Saviour, who is the Messiah, the Lord. This will be a sign for you: you will find a child wrapped in bands of cloth and lying in a manger.' And suddenly there was with the angel a multitude of the heavenly host, praising God and saying,

'Glory to God in the highest heaven,
    and on earth peace among those whom he favours!'

Reflection

Shepherds are, fittingly, the first to hear about the birth of the Lord who is our shepherd. But the 'good news of great joy' is not to be kept to themselves – it is 'for all the people'. At Christmas, we, too, can hear the great song of the angels shattering the darkness. We are filled with hope to sustain us through every human experience. And we are sent out to love and to serve.

As a professional musician working in church, I hope that the angels' song 'Glory to God in the highest heaven' can resound not just at Christ's nativity, but throughout the year. In the darkest times, light seems absent, but is present in the music we sing. Shepherds heard angels resounding 'Gloria' – and their lives were changed. May our voices and our actions convey the eternal hope of Christ's message to humankind.

Make space today to dwell on these words of Howard Thurman:
'When the song of the angels is stilled ... When the shepherds are back with their flocks, The work of Christmas begins:
To find the lost, To heal the broken ... To bring peace among the people, To make music in the heart.'

Day 4

28 DECEMBER

A Child

by Sarah Clarke

I'm a grown up. I've paid parking fines (more than I'd like to admit). Mused over wine lists (second cheapest, am I right?). Owned houseplants (RIP). Asked to speak to the manager (to my shame). I've been dull and haughty and careless and rushed and self-important and busy and tired.

Yet, at Christmas, I become a child again. Perhaps you do, too? I delight in twinkling lights and familiar carols. I eat mini chocolate angels for breakfast. I get giddy about gifts. I get giddy about the vaguest possibility of snow. I want to wear my sparkliest dress and shiniest shoes to church. I delight in the nativity story. My wide-eyed innocent joy is reawakened every December.

And, of course, it makes sense that we take on a child-like quality in this season. We're in good company: the God of the universe did it, too.

Reading Matthew 18.1-5

At that time the disciples came to Jesus and asked, 'Who is the greatest in the kingdom of heaven?' He called a child, whom he put among them, and said, 'Truly I tell you, unless you change and become like children, you will never enter the kingdom of heaven. Whoever becomes humble like this child is the greatest in the kingdom of heaven. Whoever welcomes one such child in my name welcomes me.'

Reflection

There's a simplicity to the way children interact with each other, and the world around them. They aren't deceitful or duplicitous. They say what they mean. And they ask for what they really want.

Little children don't 'network' at Christmas parties, preoccupied with rank and influence ... they have fun with the people they love. Children don't shake their head solemnly 'no thanks' at the mince pies passed around on trays, thinking of the fat content ... they receive with joy. Children don't hold grudges ... they live in the authenticity and freedom of the 'now'.

And children see beyond differences. Differences of opinion, of appearance, of politics, of background. So it's no wonder Jesus said to become (in the words of **The Message** version of the Bible) 'simple and elemental again' like a child, if those 'elements' are joy, love, trust, wonder and hope.

Is there a tradition you can bring back from your childhood this Christmas?

Something that makes you feel the wonderful, supernatural enormity of what this season is about?

29 DECEMBER

Mystery

by Bishop Rachel Treweek

As a child I loved waking on Christmas morning to find the tatty, bulging green stocking which had mysteriously appeared on my bed. With the Satsuma in the toe I knew I would find the treasure of chocolate golden coins. But apart from that I had no idea of what else lay within the misshapen fabric. How it looked and felt on the outside rarely revealed what was inside, despite my excited guesses. Things are not always what they seem.

Reading Luke 2.15-19

When the angels had left them and gone into heaven, the shepherds said to one another, 'Let us go now to Bethlehem and see this thing that has taken place, which the Lord has made known to us.' So they went with haste and found Mary and Joseph, and the child lying in the manger. When they saw this, they made known what had been told them about this child; and all who heard it were amazed at what the shepherds told them. But Mary treasured all these words and pondered them in her heart.

Reflection

An angel had unexpectedly announced to Mary a mysterious truth that she would give birth to God's Son, and spoke of thrones and greatness.

Mary must have had so many questions as well as hope and expectation about what life might be like going forward. That was surely also true of the shepherds when they too encountered mysterious angels. In the mundane and in the stuff of the ordinary, they encountered mystery and dared to enter it. Life was not as it seemed.

As Mary watched her son's life unfold, amid the miracles and mysterious stories so much didn't look very royal or world-changing, and so much was perplexing. Then came the nightmare of Jesus' torturous death. The mysterious wonder so present at the start seemed in danger of crumbling. Except there had been the pondering and treasuring all those years ago. I believe that through tears and heartache Mary did not forget: that she clung to the God who is totally other yet closer than close. She knew that how it looked and felt on the surface was not the whole picture.

Then Jesus came back to life and although the mystery was more overwhelming than ever, it was priceless treasure. A gift for us all beyond our fathoming. Death would not have the final word.

Take time today to ponder God 's love given in a tiny, vulnerable baby: fully human, fully God – Jesus Christ.

Pray that you might encounter the transforming treasure of God's love in your own life in mysterious and unexpected ways.

30 DECEMBER

Peace and Justice

by **Krish Kandiah**

A picture of three pairs of skis. A child holding a sign saying, 'Every Superhero needs a sidekick'. A man collapsed on the floor holding a pregnancy test. People choose the funniest ways to announce they are expecting a baby.

Gone are the days when a phone-around with close family and friends was enough. Now, thanks to social media, a whole new wave of creativity has been unleashed. Scanning through pictures of birth announcements you catch a sense of the joy and excitement of new parents who want the whole world to know someone is coming into their lives. The unborn child is cherished and longed for way before the actual birth.

Reading Isaiah 9.2,6-7

The people who walked in darkness have seen a great light; those who lived in a land of deep darkness – on them light has shined.... For a child has been born for us, a son given to us; authority rests upon his shoulders; and he is named Wonderful Counsellor, Mighty God, Everlasting Father, Prince of Peace. His authority shall grow continually, and there shall be endless peace for the throne of David and his kingdom. He will establish and uphold it with justice and with righteousness from this time onwards and for evermore.

Reflection

For Christians, the birth of Jesus is not revealed a mere few months but a crazy 700 years early, through the Prophet Isaiah. Times were tough then. Isaiah had a lot of bad news to pass on. God's people would lose their homes, their freedom and their security. But God did not want them to lose their hope. In the middle of a stream of doom and judgement, Isaiah posts his good news.

This child will be born to rule with justice. What good news to people oppressed and threatened by the Assyrian empire. This boy will be a wonderful counsellor. What good news to people in dire straits because of their own bad decisions. This tiny baby will be Mighty God. What good news to people suffering under an ungodly ruler. This son will be an everlasting Father. What good news to people who need nurturing with wisdom and grace. This child will be Prince of Peace. What good news to people living under constant threat of aggression and war.

Even in the middle of a world in chaos, God brings the good news of hope. Christmas reminds us of a child who came 2,000 years ago – and who will come again to fulfil those promises to a world still in chaos. He will bring justice, wisdom, nurture, and peace.

UNICEF estimates around 383,000 babies are born every day. Many are cherished and loved. But sadly too many will experience neglect, abuse, poverty and hunger.

Jesus came into the world for every one of them. What could you do or give this Christmas to help bring greater justice and security to the most vulnerable?

NEW YEAR'S EVE

Care for Those in Need

by Gina Radford

An abiding memory of 2021 is standing outside on a cold, damp day, blessing a tree planted in a care home garden as a memorial to those residents who died of COVID. Braving the elements were residents, families, friends and staff, many of whom had come in on a day off. Just one small way of making sure that we won't forget not only the sad deaths, but also the selfless and wonderful care the residents were given, mostly unseen by the outside world.

This care, these acts of kindness to some of our most vulnerable in society, has been repeated again and again all over the country during this past year.

Reading Matthew 25.34-40

'Then the king will say to those at his right hand, "Come, you that are blessed by my Father, inherit the kingdom prepared for you from the foundation of the world; for I was hungry and you gave me food, I was thirsty and you gave me something to drink, I was a stranger and you welcomed me, I was naked and you gave me clothing, I was sick and you took care of me, I was in prison and you visited me." Then the righteous will answer him, "Lord ... when was it that we saw you a stranger and welcomed you? ... And when was it that we saw you sick or in prison and visited you?" And the king will answer them, "Truly I tell you, just as you did it to one of the least of these who are members of my family, you did it to me." '

Reflection

I find myself in a dilemma at New Year's Eve. On the one hand I should be welcoming the New Year with great celebration, yet I don't want to brush the old year aside as the countdown begins. There is no doubting that 2021 has been a challenging year, and most of us look forward with hope to 2022. Yet there are some things in this last year I don't want to forget, and want to take with me into whatever the New Year brings. Chief among these is what Jesus speaks about in today's reading: those small acts of kindness and care – 'small things with great love' as Mother Teresa described them.

Whatever our feelings may be as we come to 2022, let's not forget what we learned from this past year: the importance of doing small things with great love – particularly for our most vulnerable members of society.

What do you want to bring with you from this past year into the new one?

How, practically, can you respond this year to Jesus' call for us to care for those in need?

NEW YEAR'S DAY

Giving Thanks

by **Matt Baker**

The first football match I attended was Boxing Day 1975. I don't remember much about the game except that we lost (Charlton 1 Portsmouth 3) and getting my first taste of terrace banter! However, I do remember who I was with – my family, including both Grandads, now long departed – and regardless of the result it gave a warm sense of belonging.

Christmas for me has always been a time of celebration around faith, family and football. Beginning with celebrating and giving thanks for Jesus' birth at church, then eating Christmas dinner celebrating as family followed the next day by going to the Boxing Day game together.

Reading Luke 2.15-19

The shepherds returned, glorifying and praising God for all they had heard and seen, as it had been told them. After eight days had passed, it was time to circumcise the child; and he was called Jesus, the name given by the angel before he was conceived in the womb.

When the time came for their purification according to the law of Moses, they brought him up to Jerusalem to present him to the Lord (as it is written in the law of the Lord, 'Every firstborn male shall be designated as holy to the Lord'), and they offered a sacrifice according to what is stated in the law of the Lord, 'a pair of turtle-doves or two young pigeons.'

Reflection

The shepherds returned home after that first Christmas glorifying and praising God for all that they had seen and heard. It was a time of celebration and thanksgiving. A short while later when Jesus was presented in the Temple it was a time of celebration and giving thanks for his birth.

Celebrating and giving thanks are at the heart of the Christian faith. I have been privileged to pray with footballers over the years in my role as chaplain, including one player who always insisted that we should have an 'attitude of gratitude' in our lives.

We all have different experiences and memories of Christmas past: some of those will be happy and some tinged with sadness. Christmas 2020 may have been particularly difficult as many were not able to meet with friends and family. But why not pause now and reflect on the theme of celebration and thanksgiving.

Is there a memory of a past Christmas – or a person or situation that meant a lot to you – you can now stop and give thanks to God for?

Perhaps as you pray you could also light a candle. The light can represent your prayer of thanksgiving but also an ongoing sense of gratitude for God's presence in your life.

Day 9

3 JANUARY

Rest and Restoration

by Jamie Jones-Buchanan

After 22 years of playing professional Rugby league, a game through which I both came to faith and fulfilled my boyhood dream of playing for 'The Leeds Rhinos', I retired and became an assistant coach in 2019.

Since then I have found myself having to learn all the nuances of a new trade, a new role and identity. The new job is a difficult enough at the best of times: trying to lead 30 professional athletes in the same direction, in pursuit of one mission. During the global pandemic – arguably the most calamitous time for several generations – it's been even harder. The past two years have brought many of us very little rest and no holidays – though plenty of lessons in perseverance and resilience.

I am fortunate that through this time, my relationship with my wife and our four boys within the sanctuary of our home has served both as a loving refuge and a reminder of the blessed rest that awaits us in Christ.

Reading Mark 6.30-34

The apostles gathered around Jesus, and told him all that they had done and taught. He said to them, 'Come away to a deserted place all by yourselves and rest a while.' For many were coming and going, and they had no leisure even to eat. And they went away in the boat to a deserted place by themselves. Now many saw them going and recognized them, and they hurried there on foot from all the towns and arrived ahead of them. As he went ashore, he saw a great crowd; and he had compassion for them, because they were like sheep without a shepherd; and he began to teach them many things.

Reflection

For me, Christmas is a time when so many blessings are manifest and amplified here on earth as in heaven. Wider society accepts Christmas as a holiday season, a time of joy and Christmas spirit. And a time when – even as the rest of the year seems to get busier – many people pause and regroup with friends and loved ones.

In our Bible reading today, Jesus invites his disciples to 'come away … and rest a while' with him, after weeks of endless 'coming and going'. Jesus and his disciples are seeking rest – but the story goes on to describe how crowds follow them. Tired as he is, Jesus shares with them the good news of redemption hope he came in the world to bring. And later he goes on to feed their bodies as well as their souls with five loaves and two fish. He restores them, body and soul.

Pause today and think about what Christmas means to you. Could the gifts remind you of the grace God has given to us? Could the food remind you of the spiritual bread Jesus offers? Could moments of rest remind you of the blessings of being close to Jesus?

Day 10

4 JANUARY

Carols

by Alexander Armstrong

I love that the most magical festival in our whole calendar should come in the very depths of winter.

It means the light, colour and warmth of Christmas stand out all the more starkly against that dark midwinter palette. And it makes our enjoyment so much more focused, especially when it comes to Christmas music.

There is no other season whose music we devour so hungrily, nor any that carries so many happy associations for us from down the years.

This is why it is so thrilling when we hear the first strain of Christmas music each year (the first cuckoo of Spring ain't in it).

Reading Colossians 3.16

Let the word of Christ dwell in you richly; teach and admonish one another in all wisdom; and with gratitude in your hearts sing psalms, hymns, and spiritual songs to God.

Reflection

At Christmas our churches are filled with light, warmth, togetherness, and that most special ingredient: Christmas carols.

Every year I'm so thankful for the great legacy of beautiful Christmas music we have, whether medieval, Victorian (and they were spectacularly prolific carol writers) or more recent favourites. They never fail to move me and fill me with a sense of wonder that hasn't been diluted since childhood.

Whether sung by a choir, heard drifting down high streets, or played on the radio, it feels as though we can all share in the wonder of carols at Christmas, and the comfort and hope they bring.

This Christmas, make time to listen to your favourite Christmas carols and allow the joy and the evocative memories to light up your year for you.

Why not take St Paul's advice from our reading and sing along to a carol or two today 'with gratitude in your hearts'?

Day 11

5 JANUARY

Giving and Receiving

by Tosin Oladipo

Last year at Christmas I oversaw a project to pack and distribute boxes of Christmas treats to those in need. In response to the pandemic most of the homeless and vulnerably housed had been put up in hotels and B&Bs. The project took a lot of effort logistically, and the gifts themselves were mostly unremarkable. We bought and packed treats worth around a tenner into far too big boxes. Once packed and sealed we loaded the items onto trucks then dropped them off in batches at various locations where staff panicked about where to store them. It was impersonal and (most of the time, literally) thankless.

Eventually we would receive messages of thanks, though, very rarely were they about the contents of the box – the sweets, chocolates, cans of fruit, nuts, biscuits and (for the lucky few) pairs of gloves, or socks. The messages we received were to say: thank you for remembering me – for letting me know that I am not forgotten.

Reading John 1.1-5,10-13

In the beginning was the Word, and the Word was with God, and the Word was God. He was in the beginning with God. All things came into being through him, and without him not one thing came into being. What has come into being in him was life, and the life was the light of all people. The light shines in the darkness, and the darkness did not overcome it. He was in the world, and the world came into being through him; yet the world did not know him. He came to what was his own, and his own people did not accept him. But to all who received him, who believed in his name, he gave power to become children of God …

Reflection

Many presents are unwrapped at Christmas but some it seems are truly received. Those are the best gifts of all. The ones that speak of personal connection, of understanding and of love. The act of giving becomes complete in receiving.

At this time of year, we celebrate the birth of a child who comes into the world small, helpless and unremarkable. This child is, however, the light of the world, a gift from God, and the reason we exchange gifts at Christmas. Jesus offers himself to us: the choice to receive him is entirely ours. The outcome of receiving him is life-transforming. It means receiving the priceless gift of personal connection with a loving God. At the heart of Christmas is gift – a message from God to the world, letting us know that we are not forgotten. Jesus who offers himself to all who will receive him, and in receiving lies the possibility of life in all its fullness.

In what way might you respond to the 'gift' of Jesus today?

What do you hope and pray might be transformed this Christmas?

What can you do today to remind someone that they are not forgotten?

Day 12

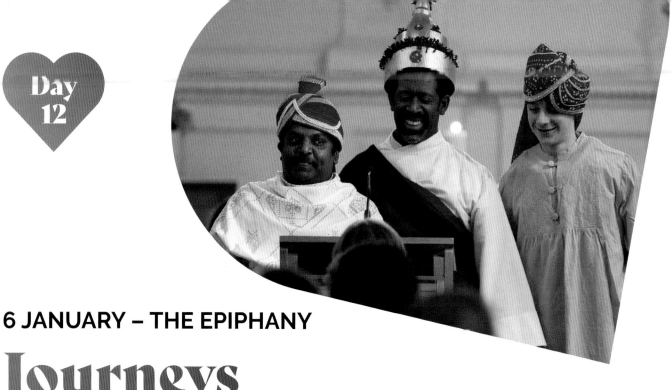

6 JANUARY – THE EPIPHANY

Journeys

by Jo Kelly-Moore

A treasure at the heart of Christmas for me each year has always been unpacking the nativity sets and setting them out, both at home and in church. The question always comes: where will we put the Wise Men? How far away should they be from the crib scene so that on this wonderful Feast of the Epiphany they get their star turn bringing their gifts to worship the Christ-child?

When our children were young the nativity sets in our house could also end up mixed up with any number of characters from Woody and Buzz to Batman entering the scene, and we would do our best not to let the Wise Men get to the manger too soon! I have always felt a bit sorry for them, too: following the star they arrive at the party just as we are packing them all up for another year!

Reading Matthew 2.9-12

When they had heard the king, the wise men set out; and there, ahead of them, went the star that they had seen at its rising, until it stopped over the place where the child was. When they saw that the star had stopped, they were overwhelmed with joy. On entering the house, they saw the child with Mary his mother; and they knelt down and paid him homage. Then, opening their treasure-chests, they offered him gifts of gold, frankincense, and myrrh. And having been warned in a dream not to return to Herod, they left for their own country by another road.

Reflection

In the story of Jesus' birth, the Magi are a wonderful 'exclamation mark' proclaiming that the light of Christ has come into the world. In following the star, they bring their lives and their gifts both to proclaim the arrival of God's Son and to worship him. As their gifts tell us something of Jesus' own life journey that was to come, so Matthew's Gospel records the Magi journeying on from Bethlehem still guided by God.

While our nativity sets are soon put away for another year, the Feast of Epiphany reminds us that the truth of Christmas never ends and that Jesus journeys on with each of us as well. He invites us to know the light of his love, joy, peace and hope guiding our way. And he invites us in turn to be bearers of his light in the world.

Where do you need to know the light of Christ's love shining into the journey of your life right now? In prayer invite Jesus to journey with you.

How can you use your gifts to bring the light of Christ's love to someone else's journey this week?

Jesus Christ is at the heart of our vision for the Church of England.

Where will a life centred on Christ take you?

We hope you have enjoyed these **#AtTheHeartOfChristmas** reflections.

Here are some possible next steps on your journey:

- Find thousands of local services and events taking place both on site and online all year round at **AChurchNearYou.com**

- Follow the Church of England on **Facebook** or subscribe to our **YouTube** channel to receive notifications of our national online services.

- Visit **churchofengland.org** to sign up for and take part in campaigns and initiatives from the Church of England in 2022 and beyond – including our 2022 Lent journey exploring the theme of justice.

- Visit **CofE.io/DailyPrayer** to join the hundreds of thousands of people who have made a pattern of prayer part of their everyday lives using our free Daily Prayer app and audio services.